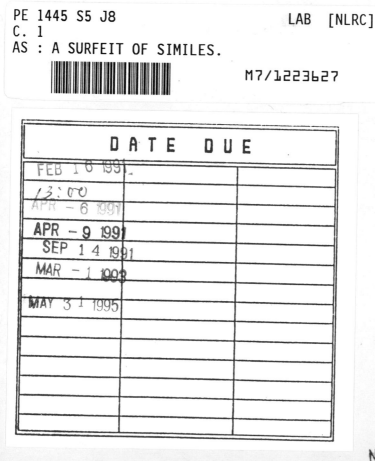

A SURFEIT
OF SIMILES

A SURFEIT
OF SIMILES

NORTON JUSTER

PICTURES BY
DAVID SMALL

WILLIAM MORROW & COMPANY, INC.
NEW YORK

Library of Congress Cataloging-in-Publication Data

Juster, Norton.
As : a surfeit of similes / by Norton Juster :
pictures by David Small.
p.   cm.
Summary: Defines the mode of comparison known as simile and
provides many examples in rhyming text.
ISBN 0-688-08139-8.   ISBN 0-688-08140-1 (lib. bdg.)
1. Simile—Juvenile literature.   2. English language—Comparison—
Juvenile literature.   3. English language—Terms and phrases—
Juvenile literature.   [1. Simile.   2. English language—Terms and
phrases.]   I. Small, David, ill.   II. Title.   III. Title:
Surfeit of Similes.
PE1445.S5J8 1989
808—dc19   88-8449   CIP   AC

For Allison and Eric,
as shiny as pearls

"What's a simile?"

"Isn't it one of those spicy sausages you put on a sandwich?"

"That's a salami."

"I thought Salami was that lady who cut off John the Baptist's head. They say that when she danced, she was as graceful as a willow."

"That was Salome, and I think that's a simile."
"It is? Can we do that again?"

As poor as a church mouse
As thin as a rail

As smooth as a porpoise
As rough as a gale

As brave as a lion
As spry as a cat
As bright as a penny
As weak as a rat

As proud as a peacock
As sly as a fox

As mad as a hatter
As strong as an ox

As fair as a lily
As empty as air
As fresh as a daisy
As cross as a bear

As round as an apple
As hot as the mustard
As cunning as snakes
As creamy as custard

As firm as a melon
As brown as a berry
As fresh as a peach
As black as a cherry

PSST! WANNA BUY A SIMILE?

As pure as an angel
As clever as zippers
As awkward as crutches
As friendly as slippers

As hard as a rock
As white as a sheet
As sweet as a lute
As red as a beet

As light as a feather
As wrinkled as prunes
As stiff as a poker
Elusive as tunes

As creepy as spiders
As harsh as a snub
As cheerful as bluebirds
As warm as a tub

As moist as the dew
As quiet as pride
Uncertain as weather
As sure as the tide

As sharp as a stick
As due as the rent
As foul as a sty

"Of course you have to be careful what you compare things to."

"How big is your elephant?"
"Very big."
"How big?"
"Very, very big!"
"That doesn't seem so big."
"I mean very, very, very big—like really big!"
"How big is that?"
"As big as you can get!"
"I'm still not sure."

"AS BIG AS YOUR HOUSE!"

"Thanks, but I live in a very small house. Would you like to try again?"

As flat as a pancake

As warm as your socks

As dead as a doornail

As constant as clocks

As patient as lizards
As heavy as lead
As slow as the ketchup
As safe as your bed

As serious as checkers
As cozy as kittens
As short as bad tempers
As lost as your mittens

As still as a statue
As busy as bees
As scary as heights
As silly as knees

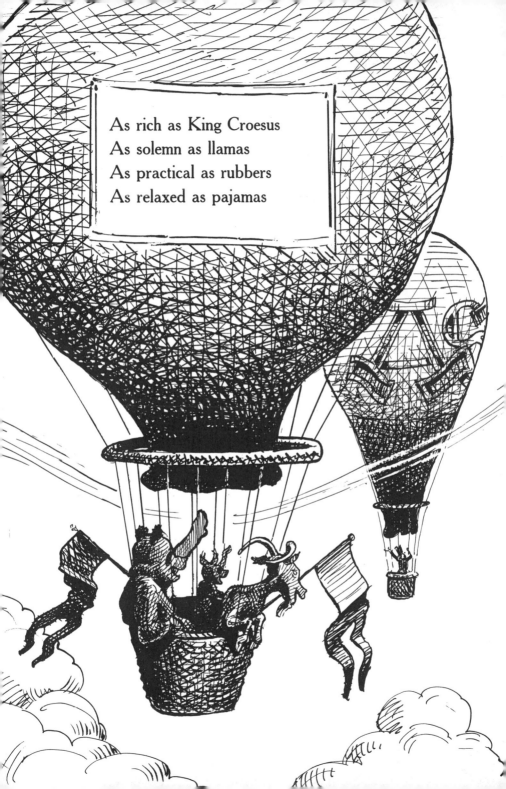

As rich as King Croesus
As solemn as llamas
As practical as rubbers
As relaxed as pajamas

As lazy as summer
As useless as foyers
As solemn as judges
As cautious as lawyers

As salty as kippers
As bright as the morning
As fit as a fiddle
As cool as an awning

As proud as a parent
As plump as corn fritters
As blunt as the truth
As dull as no-hitters

"Sometimes, what something isn't—can tell you a lot about what it is. . . ."

As comfortable as a hairbrush in bed
As graceful as a hippopotamus on roller skates
As clean as a coal miner's fingernails

As convenient as an unabridged dictionary
As reassuring as a dentist's smile
As exciting as a plateful of cabbage

As pleasant as ice water in your shoe
As welcome as a rainy Saturday
As easy as collecting feathers in a hurricane

"Gee, thanks. That's as interesting as the magazines in a doctor's waiting room. Do you have any more?"

As fierce as a leopard

As drunk as a sailor

As noisy as starlings
As grim as a jailer

As submerged as a sub
As many as guppies

As prickly as thistles
As sick as a dog

As tight as a suture
As fat as a hog

As spicy as gossip
Alike as green peas

As mysterious as stew
As smelly as cheese

As brittle as crackers
As deaf as a post
As twisted as pretzels
As crisp as the toast

As boring as uncles
As grave as morticians
As dreadful as funerals
As strong as traditions

As helpful as boy scouts
As long as a train
As cruel as a hoax
As clogged as a drain

As faint as a whisper
As certain as Christmas
Contagious as yawning
As slim as an isthmus

"But you can overdo it."
"I can't see a thing!"
"It's as dark as a vampire's shadow."
"As dark as an undiscovered cave."
"As dark as the back of a beetle."
"As dark as a dreadful superstition."
"As dark as midnight at the bottom of a well."
"As dark as a miser's pocketbook."
"As dark as the woods when you're lost."
"As dark as a terrible secret."
"That's funny, I just can't see it. It must be too dark. Let's just keep going."
AS

As blind as a bat

As queer as a duck

As different as noses
As fickle as luck

As still as a corpse
As sharp as a sleuth

As old as some jokes
As far as Duluth

As wise as an owl
As sure as prediction

As useless as warts
As true as good fiction

As smart as a whip
As neat as a pin

As dear as a dolly
As ugly as sin

As stubborn as laces
As grim as a drought
As rude as the garlic
As sauer as kraut

As kind as grandparents
As persistent as creditors
As gnawing as doubt
As picky as editors

As varied as snowflakes
As handy as tacks
As thrilling as danger
Unlikely as yaks

As expected as presents
As deep as true love
As uncertain as graduates
As snug as your glove

As lively as polkas
As contrary as kites
As meager as praise
As precious as rights

As tempting as elsewhere
As delicate as lace
As full as a tick
As fast as a chase

As vague as a longing
As destructive as time
As angry as hornets
As relentless as rhyme

As brittle as glass
As tight as a screw
As gentle as caring
And as sad as "Adieu"

"You see, it's really quite simple. A simile is just a mode of comparison employing *as* and *like* to reveal the hidden character or essence of whatever we want to describe, and through the use of fancy, association, contrast, extension, or imagination, to enlarge our understanding or perception of human experience and observation."

"Of course! It's as clear as a bell! Now, what's a surfeit?"

Spotlight Club Mysteries
by Florence Parry Heide
and Sylvia Worth Van Clief

•

THE MYSTERY OF THE SILVER TAG
THE MYSTERY OF THE MISSING SUITCASE
THE HIDDEN BOX MYSTERY
MYSTERY AT MACADOO ZOO

A Spotlight Club Mystery

The
Hidden Box
Mystery

Florence Parry Heide
and Sylvia Worth Van Clief

Illustrations by Seymour Fleishman

ALBERT WHITMAN & Company, Chicago

Library of Congress Cataloging in Publication Data

Heide, Florence Parry.
  The hidden box mystery.

  (Their A Spotlight Club mystery)   (Pilot books series)
  SUMMARY: A series of petty thefts in the neighborhood
leads the Spotlight Club into a new mystery.
  [1. Mystery stories]   I. Van Clief, Sylvia Worth,
joint author.   II. Fleishman, Seymour, illus.
III. Title.
PZ7.H36Hi   [Fic]   72-13351
ISBN 0-8075-3270-3

Contents

THE HIDDEN BOX MYSTERY

1 · Sneak Thief in Town

JAY COULD HARDLY believe his eyes. What was a police car doing in front of the Cooper house?

Was there another robbery in the neighborhood?

Jay ran up the porch steps to put Coopers' newspaper in the slot in the door. They always wanted it that way.

The policeman was just leaving.

"Sorry, ma'am," the policeman was saying. "This is the third little robbery this week. We're doing all we can."

Mrs. Cooper came to the door. She was wearing rollers in her hair.

"I can't believe it," she said. "I had just gone to the store. Someone must have walked right in the front door! What nerve! And he took that conch shell we got in Florida. I had just dusted it before I left. When I came back, it was gone from the coffee table."

The policeman sighed. "A sneak thief, that's what it is, Mrs. Cooper. We've had several complaints. But so far the thief hasn't taken anything of value."

"Of value?" cried Mrs. Cooper. "That conch shell was on our coffee table for five years! Who knows when we'll get another?"

"Sorry," said the policeman. He shrugged and walked down the porch steps. Jay followed him.

"Did you say a sneak thief?" asked Jay.

The policeman glanced at Jay and nodded absently.

"Well, maybe I can help," Jay said.

"Sure, fella. You're a newsboy. You get around. Keep your eyes and ears open. Maybe you will see something. Or hear something." He winked at Jay.

"Yes, *sir,*" Jay said eagerly. "It's just the kind of thing we can do."

The policeman stopped on the bottom step and looked over at Jay. "We?" he asked, smiling.

"My friends," explained Jay. "Well, one friend and one sister. We have a sort of detective club. I'm Jay Temple. My sister's Cindy. Dexter Tate is the other member."

The policeman nodded. "Okay," he said. "My name's Hap Brady. Call me at headquarters if you have anything to report. Anyone who is acting strange or anyone new in the neighborhood. Something like that."

"You bet, officer," said Jay.

Jay raced on to the next house. He was walking, not riding his bike. He tossed the newspaper on the porch and ran on. He kept thinking all the time. Another mystery for the Spotlight Club! A sneak thief to catch!

At the third house Jay's eye fell on a ten-speed silver bicycle. It was parked in front of the Katz house. Only it wasn't the Katz house anymore, Jay thought. The Crumps had rented it a month ago.

"Boy!" said Jay under his breath. He stopped and looked at the bike. "Wouldn't it be great to use that on my newspaper route instead of my old bike —up for repairs again!"

He sighed to himself.

As Jay was tossing the paper up on the porch, Mr. Crump came jogging around the house in his sweatsuit. His thin hair was plastered to his head, and his long thin nose was dripping. He saw Jay, and wiped his forehead.

"Hey, Jay," he said. He smiled, and his smile took up half his face. He treated Jay as if he'd known him for years. "Hey, Jay, whaddya say, what's the newest news today?"

Jay smiled. This was the way Mr. Crump always talked.

"Gee, Mr. Crump, have you heard about the robberies in the neighborhood? It looks as if there's a sneak thief around. He took something today, at the Coopers, down the street. Just a conch shell, but Mrs. Cooper's upset about it. The policeman asked me to keep an eye on things." Jay looked proud.

"Say, that's funny," said Mr. Crump, wiping his nose on his sleeve. "We missed our pepper mill today. I thought Bertha had just mislaid it. But she'd gone shopping, and I was out on my bike, and—" He shrugged and shook his head. "Guess you can't trust anybody."

"Say, that's some bike you have," said Jay.

"You bet," said Mr. Crump. "A bike ride a day keeps the doctor away. I cycle, I jog, I eat the right things. A fella's got to keep in shape, right? Right."

He looked over at Jay. "Too bad, having to worry about a sneak thief in this nice neighborhood. One reason we moved here. Safe. I'll tell Bertha. We'll have to lock the house up after this, I guess."

Randy, the neighborhood pet, tail wagging, came bounding up to Jay. "Say," said Mr. Crump, "is that a neighborhood dog? He seems so friendly."

"Nicest dog around," said Jay, bending down to pat Randy. "Lives in that big house up on the corner."

"We always keep our bones for nice dogs," said Mr. Crump.

"Then he'll be your friend for life," laughed Jay. "I'll see you later, Mr. Crump. I've got to tell my friends about the robberies. It's a real mystery for us to work on."

"Hey, you're my pal, call me Cal," said Mr.

Crump. "Cal and Bertha. That's us, plain folks. No mister- and missus-ing us. No fuss. That's us."

"Okay," said Jay, and he hurried off.

As soon as he'd delivered his last paper, Jay raced home. As he walked in the door, he heard his sister Cindy on the telephone.

"Oh, Mom, really! We still have all day tomorrow to do it. School doesn't start again till the day after. And you know how fast we are about writing papers, once we get started. We're going over to the museum tomorrow to do our research. Relax, Mom. We haven't flunked yet."

Jay motioned to Cindy that he wanted to talk to her. Cindy motioned to Jay that she was ready to talk.

"Yes, I'll put the roast in the oven. Yes, right now. It will be done when you get home from work. Okay. Bye."

Cindy hung up. "I love our mother," she said. "We have to save her from her worries. What's up?"

"Everything," said Jay. "But now you make *me* worry. What's this about writing a paper?"

"You'll remember when you remember that *school* starts day after tomorrow," said Cindy.

Jay groaned. "Don't tell me. I remember. We have to do that paper."

Cindy made a deep bow. "You are right, Great Brain. And now for the next question: When are we going to do it?"

"Later," said Jay. "Right now we've got something really important to do. Solve a mystery! The Spotlight Club to the rescue!"

"I wish we could go to a mystery-solving school," said Cindy.

"This is important," said Jay impatiently. "Where's Dexter?"

Cindy pointed. "In his own house, awaiting thy call."

"Let's go over there. Then I can tell you both at the same time," said Jay.

"Okay," said Cindy, jumping up. "But I promised Mom I'd throw the roast in the oven first. I'll be right there. Don't say anything till I come."

"Well, hurry," said Jay, running out the door.

He rang the Tates' doorbell and walked in. That was their system. It saved anyone having to answer the doorbell.

"Hey, Dexter!" he bellowed.

Dexter yelled from upstairs, "Be right down!"

In a moment Dexter was running down the stairs, holding his glasses in one hand.

Dexter was just putting his glasses on when Cindy rang the doorbell and walked in.

"That was fast," said Jay. "You must have really thrown that roast in the oven."

"I didn't want to miss anything," said Cindy breathlessly.

"Hope you didn't miss the oven," laughed Dexter.

"This is important," said Jay. "There was another robbery today, at the Coopers. And I saw Mr. Crump. They had a robbery, too. And the policeman at Coopers, Hap Brady, asked me to call in if I spotted anything strange. That's a perfect job for the Spotlight Club. I told him we'd keep our eyes open."

"Keep our eyes open?" asked Dexter. "You mean *we* will solve the mystery."

"Well, yes, of course we will," said Jay. "But I didn't want to hurt his feelings. Policemen like to think they're really doing the main job."

Just then Anne, Dexter's older sister, flung the front door open and ran inside.

"Honestly," she said. "Isn't anything safe any more? Even in broad daylight?"

"What are you talking about?" asked Dexter.

"Sally's car was just robbed. It happened while we were waiting to play tennis over in Random Park."

The three Spotlight Club members stared at Anne.

"Where were you? What happened?" asked Jay.

The three detectives gathered around Anne.

"Sally and I had gone to play tennis over at Random Park. It was crowded. We were waiting for the court."

"Where was the car?" asked Dexter.

"Right in the parking lot. Our backs were

turned. Anybody could have done it," said Anne. "And the thief didn't take much. Some old tennis balls. And some things Sally had just bought at the drugstore."

"Did you see anyone?" asked Cindy.

"Everyone," said Anne. "Lots of kids. Old people walking around. People on bikes, an old man feeding the birds, a lady with rollers in her hair. Can you tell me why anyone would be *seen* with rollers?" She shook her head. "A couple of workmen on a coffee break. I told you, the park was crowded."

"You'd make a good Spotlight Club member," said Jay. "You really noticed a lot."

"Well, I didn't notice the important thing— who did it," said Anne.

"When did it happen?" asked Dexter.

"Just a few minutes ago. Sally was all upset. She just dropped me off and went home."

Anne went into the hall and picked up the telephone. "I've got to call everyone," she said.

"And we've got to find the sneak thief," said Cindy. "He seems to be all over the town."

"A conch shell, a pepper mill, some old tennis balls," said Jay. "It doesn't make sense."

"How can we go about finding him?" Dexter wondered out loud.

"Let's call him Mr. X," suggested Cindy.

"Hap Brady, the policeman, said to watch for strangers or for someone acting suspiciously. Anything different," said Jay.

"Maybe we can spot someone *taking* something. How about that?" said Dexter. "And maybe Mr. X is taking something right now. Let's go out and look around. We still have plenty of time before supper."

"We do," laughed Cindy. "That roast was frozen solid. I forgot to take it out of the freezer."

"Let's take our bikes," said Dexter.

"Mine's in getting a new wheel," said Jay.

"Then we'll all walk," said Dexter.

"I've got my notebook in my sweater pocket," said Cindy. "I'm ready."

They started off to search for clues.

In their search the three Spotlight Club members separated, met, and separated again. By supper-time they had found nothing—not a single clue.

"We have all day tomorrow," said Dexter.

"Remember those papers we've got to write. School starts day after tomorrow," said Cindy. "We've got to get to the museum to do the research for them. And the museum closes at three tomorrow."

Jay groaned. "That's the trouble with long spring vacations. You forget that school is ever going to come again."

"It's the last time I'll ever leave anything till the last minute," grumbled Dexter.

"Want to bet?" grinned Jay.

"Well, it won't be too bad," said Cindy. "We've all got the same questions to answer. And the same exhibit to look at. The Early American one. We can help each other. That way it will go fast."

"It's for some paper Mr. Hobson is writing, isn't it?" asked Dexter, pushing his glasses up on his forehead.

Cindy nodded.

"We're doing all this for his paper? What's he ever done for us?" complained Jay.

"Well, he's been a pretty nice principal, for one thing," said Cindy. "Everyone in the school is supposed to do it."

"He'd better give us all A's, that's all I can say," said Dexter. "I'll run up and get the assignment. Just a sec."

He ran upstairs and was back in a moment waving a paper. He fixed his glasses and read: "What objects can you find in the Early American Exhibit that help you understand the way Americans then lived? Pick one object and contrast it with a similar object in today's world."

Jay groaned. "I can't do it," he said.

"Oh, it's easy," said Cindy. "We just have to write a page. Why don't we work on the mystery until noon and then meet at the museum?"

"Okay," said Jay. "Then we'll still have most of the afternoon to work on finding Mr. X."

"He may be stealing something right at this very moment," said Cindy. "We've got to find him quickly."

"We will," said Dexter firmly.

22

2 · Cindy Meets the Birdman

DEXTER CALLED Jay early the next morning. "Now hear this. The sneak thief has struck again," he announced. "I'm coming over to tell you about it. We'll have to start looking for him right now."

In a moment Dexter ran up Temples' front steps.

"What happened?" asked Jay.

Cindy ran in from the kitchen. "What did he take?"

"The Peabodys were out playing bridge last night," said Dexter breathlessly. "While they were gone, the sneak thief stole all the ashtrays from their front porch."

"Ashtrays, a conch shell, a pepper mill, tennis balls," said Jay, frowning. "Nothing seems to fit."

"When we find Mr. X we can ask him," laughed Cindy.

"Okay, we're splitting up," said Dexter. "Let's see who finds him first!"

"I'll meet you at twelve on the museum steps, okay?" asked Cindy.

"Twelve sharp," said Jay. And the three detectives parted company.

Cindy hadn't found a single clue to the robberies by the end of the morning. She climbed the front steps of the museum.

The boys hadn't come yet. She must be early, she thought. She looked at her watch. She wasn't early. They were late. As usual.

Cindy walked around to the gate to the museum park. She glanced up at the steps that led into the museum from the park. No boys. She looked around the park.

At the end of the park was a pond, and Cindy could see white swans swimming in the water. She decided to walk down to look at them.

She passed the big fountain and walked all around it, looking at the statue. The walk around the fountain was being repaired. A workman was busy. There were lots of pennies on the bottom of the fountain.

"People always throw pennies in fountains for good luck," she thought. "Guess I will too. I'll need some luck. On the mystery, and on the paper we've got to write."

Cindy found a penny in her pocket and threw it in. "Good luck to you, penny, and good luck to me, Cindy," she said to herself. Then she walked down the slope to the pond.

Standing on the edge of the pond, next to a shopping cart, stood a little old man. He was feeding the swans. His shopping cart was filled with loaves of bread, long loaves of French bread in paper bags.

"He must make lots of sandwiches or feed lots of birds," thought Cindy, walking over to watch him.

The man turned around and smiled. He had bright blue eyes that twinkled. It was a warm day, but he wore a red woolen cap pulled down over his ears.

"Good morning, miss, and a good day to you," he said. "Are you interested in birds?"

"Yes, but I don't know much about them," said Cindy. "And I don't know anything at all about swans."

The man made a little clicking noise with his tongue. Two of the swans glided over to the edge of the pond.

"See? They're my friends," said the old man. "I always feed them, in wintertime when they're in the zoo, and then here in the spring, when they are put back in this pond. I think the swans like this place better. But it always takes them a while to get used to it. Seeing me makes them feel at home again."

He watched as the swans came closer.

"This is Albert," said the little old man. "And this is Einstein."

"Do they really have names?" asked Cindy. "They all look the same to me."

"They get names the same way people do," smiled the man. "If you give someone a name, it's his name from then on."

"My name's Cindy Temple," said Cindy.

"And I'm the Birdman," said the old man. "Everyone calls me that. It's enough of a name, I guess. My real name is Ezra Zebediah Quayle, so Birdman is easier."

"Hello, Birdman," said Cindy. She thought to herself, "What a nice, kind man."

The Birdman made his little clicking noise and a couple of other swans edged closer.

"These are Rose and Thorn," he said. "They get cranky once in a while, just like human beings. Try feeding them. Just take a bit of bread from the cart."

He saw Cindy looking at the shopping cart. "I buy day-old bread at the Elm Street Bakery," he explained. "I feed these swans here at the museum, the pigeons at the library and the courthouse, and

27

the sparrows at Random Park. And a lot of other birds all over the place. They all know me. We're friends."

Suddenly Cindy heard Dexter's whistle. She looked around. The two boys were standing on the museum steps, waving.

She turned back to the Birdman. "I've got to go," she said. "Good-bye, and say good-bye to Albert and Einstein. And Rose and Thorn."

She ran up the slope to the museum steps.

"Girls are always late," said Dexter as Cindy ran up the steps.

"Girls are always early," said Cindy. "That way they have time to have an adventure while they're waiting for the boys, who are always late."

"Let's get this museum thing over so we can go back to our search for clues," said Jay.

"I didn't find a single clue all morning," said Cindy.

"Neither did we," said Dexter. "But we will. Now, which way to the Early American Exhibit?"

"There's a sign," said Jay. They walked toward

the exhibit. "Hey, it's pretty crowded. It looks as if the whole school waited until today to take a look."

"The whole school and every ladies' club in town," said Dexter. "How can we get close enough to see anything?"

"Push," said Jay.

"Ooze," said Cindy. "It's more polite."

The three were finally close enough to see the exhibit. They looked at old oil lamps, at a loom, at baby cradles, muskets, clothes, and much more.

"Where's Dexter?" asked Jay after a few minutes.

"Lost in the shuffle, I guess," said Cindy.

In a few minutes Dexter shoved his way through the crowd to find Cindy and Jay. "Hey, come on over here to the other end of the hall," he said. "There's a great chess set over there."

"Chess set?" asked Jay.

"Yeah, it isn't in this exhibit. It's at the other end, in a sort of alcove. It's really neat," said Dexter.

"Well, I'll go and look at it if it isn't crowded," said Jay. "I feel like a sardine."

"There's not a soul there," said Dexter. "Come on. Want to come, Cindy?"

"Sure," she said, putting her notebook and pencil in her sweater pocket. "I've seen all I need to for ten papers."

"Good, you can help me with mine then," said Dexter. "All I've seen is the chess set, and it isn't even Early American. It's Chinese. But it's something."

The Spotlight Club members threaded their way through the crowd and along an empty hall.

"There it is," said Dexter, pointing behind a velvet rope to a chessboard set up on an ornate table. The chess pieces were made of jade, beautifully carved. Each piece was a little work of art. A sign said, "Loaned by B. Thorndyke."

"Remember last summer when your Uncle Jim tried to teach us to play chess?" asked Jay.

"All I remember about it is kings, queens, jacks," said Cindy.

"Silly, there aren't any jacks in chess. It's kings, queens, knights, bishops, rooks, and pawns," said Dexter, leaning over to look at the chess set.

"Here! What are you up to?" asked a high shrill voice.

The three Spotlight Club members turned around to see a thin, sharp-nosed woman frowning at them. She wore a guard's badge on her plain blue dress. She had come up without a sound because she wore sneakers.

"We're just looking at this chess set," said Dexter. His smile faded as he saw the woman's angry frown.

"This is a very special exhibit," she said, looking suspiciously at the three detectives. "It's been loaned to the museum by Mr. Benjamin Thorndyke. He has that big estate at the other end of town. He didn't lend it to the museum just to have kids monkeying around with it, I can tell you."

Cindy bristled. "We weren't monkeying around," she said. "We were just looking at it."

The thin lady sniffed and tucked a stray strand of hair in the net she was wearing.

"I've never seen a kid yet who could look without touching," she said. "And my job is to see that nothing happens to anything here. That set ought to be in a glass case. Then you couldn't touch it."

"We're not touching it," said Jay.

"Mr. Thorndyke never let anyone touch it. Except me. I was his personal secretary." She sniffed again. "Then his cousin started coming around. He got my job. It wasn't fair. Just because he was related, he got the job. Anyway, I was there a long time. Long enough to know Mr. Thorndyke and his ways. And he never did like children in his house. Not ever. Neither did I."

Jay sighed. "Come on, gang," he said. "I've seen enough anyway."

"Don't you hate people who think all kids are awful?" asked Dexter as they made their way through the crowd and outside.

"Oh, well, let's forget it and get back to our mystery. We won't find anything exciting around here," said Jay.

"You could be so wrong," said Cindy.

And Dexter was wrong. Dead wrong.

3 · Mighty Mysterious

THE BIRDMAN was walking toward the three detectives as they ran down the museum steps.

"Hello again, Birdman!" called Cindy. "How are Albert and Einstein?"

The Birdman waved to Cindy and smiled.

"Who are Albert and Einstein? And who's that?" whispered Jay.

"One of these days you'll realize that every time you're late I meet all kinds of interesting people," Cindy whispered back.

When they came up to the Birdman, Cindy introduced Jay and Dexter.

"Where are Albert and Einstein?" asked Dexter.

"Oh, they're swimming in the pond," laughed Cindy.

The Birdman parked his shopping cart next to the bicycle rack, where several bicycles were parked.

"I'm going in for a drink of water," he explained. "Lots of water everywhere, but just for swans and fish." He smiled and climbed the museum steps.

"What's all this in his cart?" asked Dexter. "Bread?"

"He feeds the birds," explained Cindy. "All over town."

"You mean he just walks all around with old bread? Sounds nutty to me," said Jay.

"He likes the birds, and the birds like him," Cindy explained. "I think it's nice there are people like that around. He feeds the swans here, and the sparrows in Random Park, and. . ."

"Hey," said Dexter, pulling his glasses down on his nose. "Random Park. That's where Anne and Sally were when Sally's car was robbed yesterday."

"Wait a minute!" exclaimed Jay. "Remember? She said there was an old guy feeding birds!"

"Oh, stop," said Cindy. "That sweet old guy isn't your Mr. X. Just because we're working on a mystery, we don't have to suspect everyone."

"Yes, we do," said Jay. "Because that's the only way we can get a list of suspects. We can put him on our list of suspects. Then if we prove he isn't the one, we can cross him off, see? The Birdman goes first on the list. You said he goes all over town —well, the robberies are all over town."

"He's not going on any list of mine," said Cindy.

"Then you're not being a true detective," said Jay.

"He probably isn't the one, Cindy, but we should put him down, anyway," said Dexter.

"Not me," said Cindy.

As they were arguing, a gruff voice said, "Okay, kids, you gotta move out of here. We're starting repairs. Didn't you see the sign? Can't you read?"

As they turned around, a big burly man stepped off the museum steps. He walked toward the three detectives. He pointed back to a sign that read: CLOSING FOR REPAIRS, 3 O'CLOCK.

"I can read," said Cindy, upset by the man's gruffness. "And I can tell time, too. It's not even two o'clock."

"I just was in checking with the museum director," said the big man. "He said to close everything down *now*. The museum, the park, the works. They're already ringing the buzzer in there to get everyone out—now."

A tall thin man in white overalls ran up to the big man. "Mr. Grubbs," he said, "the sod's here."

"Okay," said Mr. Grubbs. "And we've still got to get ready to pour the new cement around the fountain. All we need is some kids getting in the way. Start moving, you three. Scat!"

Mr. Grubbs walked off toward the pond. The man in white overalls followed him.

"Talk about an old crab!" said Cindy. "That's two in a row. That thin lady in the museum and that big man out here."

She turned around and saw the Birdman walking down the museum steps. He was frowning. He didn't notice Cindy.

"Hey, Birdman!" said Cindy, smiling. At least that's one friendly person around here, she thought.

The Birdman jumped and looked around, startled. He saw Cindy, stood still a moment, and then looked behind him. Then he walked over to Cindy.

"Is there anything wrong?" asked Cindy.

The Birdman shook his head and glanced over his shoulder at the museum.

"No, there's nothing wrong. Well, yes there is. I just said 'Good afternoon, ma'am,' to that Miss Lampkins in there. She's the lady guard. Miss Agnes Lampkins."

"Yes, we just met her," said Cindy.

The Birdman went on. "She was all upset about something. She barked at me for taking a drink of water. I hate to have people yell at me, that's all. Her voice goes right through me."

Cindy and the boys nodded. "She's really some-thing," said Cindy.

38

The Birdman glanced at his cart. "I've got to go along now," he said. He spoke quickly. "The birds are waiting."

Cindy turned to the boys, who had been watching the Birdman. "Talking about water makes me thirsty," she said.

"Me, too," said Jay. "Let's go in and get a drink before the museum closes."

"Okay," said Dexter. "Hope we don't run into that Agnes Lampkins."

They found the water fountain right next to the chess set.

"That old dragon Lampkins isn't around," said Jay, looking over his shoulder. "Good."

Cindy took a swallow. "Warm," she commented. "But wet."

"Good enough for me," said Jay. He was just leaning over to drink when Dexter exclaimed, "Hey! Look! Two of the chess pieces are missing. Someone's stolen them."

4 · Mr. X Strikes Again

JAY AND CINDY ran over to Dexter.

"Stolen? What? Where?" asked Cindy, looking around the museum quickly.

"Right there—a king and a knight," said Dexter. "All the pieces were right on the board when we were here before."

"Then they've just been stolen in the last few minutes," said Jay. "That means . . ." He stopped and thought. "It means," he said slowly, "that who-ever took them must be in the building."

"Or might have left the building just in the last few minutes," said Dexter. "Mr. X strikes again! It must have been that sneak thief."

"We've got to report the missing pieces. Right now," said Cindy. "Maybe the museum people could search everyone who's still here. That way they could find the thief."

"Thief? What thief?" cried a shrill voice. It was Agnes Lampkins hurrying over to them in her sloppy sneakers.

"Two chessmen have been stolen," said Dexter.

Agnes Lampkins stared at the chessboard. Then she turned on Dexter and Jay and Cindy.

"If anything's missing, my guess is that you took it yourselves," she snapped.

"We were just going to report it," said Cindy. "Let's go, gang."

"Oh, no you don't!" said Agnes Lampkins to Cindy. Cindy had the curious feeling that maybe Agnes Lampkins was going to shake her.

"You'll report nothing," she said. "I'll report it through the proper channels. Mr. Thorndyke has to know first. He hates rumors and publicity. I worked for him once, you know. You run on. I'll report it to the proper persons. I'm just leaving." She pointed to her sweater and her bulky purse.

Cindy stared at Agnes Lampkins and then looked at the boys. Could they trust this strange woman to report the theft?

"Let's go, gang," said Jay suddenly, turning on his heel.

Dexter and Cindy followed him.

"She must have swiped the chessmen," whispered Jay. "We've got to report them missing before we leave. We can't be sure she will if she took them."

Dexter looked over his shoulder. Agnes Lampkins was leaving the museum by the park door.

"Looks as if you're right, Jay," said Dexter. "She's just left—without reporting anything."

"Come on, let's find another guard," said Cindy.

"I just want to take a look at what she's up to," said Dexter.

He ran back and looked out a window that

faced on the museum park. He adjusted his glasses and looked again.

The Birdman hadn't left the park yet. He was leaning over, looking into the fountain. As Dexter watched, the Birdman took something from his pocket. He leaned over and carefully placed it in the fountain. Was it a penny for good luck? Or was it one of the chessmen?

As Dexter watched, Mr. Grubbs, the big burly workman, came over to the Birdman and said something. The Birdman looked up, startled. Then he walked quickly away from the fountain. He got his cart and started out of the park. Mr. Grubbs closed the park gates.

"Hey, come on, Dex, hurry. We've got to report the theft!" called Jay.

"Yeah," said Dexter thoughtfully.

What had the Birdman put in the fountain? And where was Agnes Lampkins?

Dexter turned and followed Jay and Cindy.

By the time the three saw another guard, the museum was almost empty. It was too late to search anyone, thought Cindy. Whoever had taken the chess pieces must be gone.

They hurried over to a tall thin guard with long hair. He was telling everyone that the museum was closing.

The three detectives quickly told the guard about their discovery. He nodded and pursed his lips as he listened.

"You've got to do something!" said Jay. "There's been a sneak thief taking things all over town. Who knows what he'll take next?"

"Maybe you could search the people who are still here," said Dexter.

The guard shook his head. "No, I couldn't do that. Even if the museum director were here. And he's not in town today. Even he probably couldn't do that. But I'll call the police right away. It's lucky you kids noticed the pieces were missing. With the museum closing early, we wouldn't have found out until tomorrow."

The guard reached into his pocket. "Here," he said. "Write your names and addresses down. The museum director will certainly want to thank you. It's the first time anything's been stolen from here."

The three detectives wrote their names in the guard's notebook. Then they left the museum by the front door on the street side. The park was already closed.

As they walked down the street, they talked about the mystery of the missing chess pieces.

"I don't think it was Mr. X, the sneak thief," said Cindy thoughtfully. "He just takes things like shells and ashtrays. He hasn't taken anything valuable."

"You're right, Cindy," said Dexter. "These chess pieces are really valuable."

"I think it was Agnes Lampkins," said Jay. "It has to be. She had plenty of chance to take the chess pieces. And she knows what they are worth."

"Yes, and she sounds as if she'd like to get even with old Mr. Thorndyke," said Cindy. "Remember he fired her and made his cousin his secretary. She was mad about that."

"Wait a minute," said Dexter slowly. "There's

something else funny. Something about the Birdman. I saw him putting something in the fountain. It might have been one of the chessmen."

"Or it might have been a penny," said Cindy.

"He went in to get a drink of water. And he came out all upset about something, remember?" said Dexter. "Maybe he was going to take all the pieces and Agnes Lampkins came by."

"Oh, don't be silly. He wouldn't take a thing," said Cindy.

"Don't be so sure, Cindy," Dexter warned.

"Look, there he is now, up ahead," said Jay.

"Let's catch up with him," said Cindy. "If you get to know him you'll see that he couldn't be Mr. X."

Dexter poked Jay as Cindy ran ahead. "Let's keep an eye on him, anyway. If we could have gone back into the park—we could have tried to see what the Birdman put in the fountain."

"We'll find a way," Jay said.

Suddenly the boys heard a bicycle horn. They turned around. Jay waved. It was Cal Crump. He pulled up beside the boys.

"Hi, Mr. Crump," said Jay. "Guess what happened?"

"Hey, Jay, I'm your pal, call me Cal," said Cal Crump. He got off his bike and pulled it up on the sidewalk. "Hey, Jay, I saw you at the exhibit.

Tried to wave to you. Wanted to show you that old bike. A real old-timer. One big wheel and two baby ones. Darndest thing I ever saw."

"There was a robbery at the museum!" said Jay. "Two valuable chess pieces were stolen."

"You're kidding!" said Cal Crump.

At that moment the boys and Cal Crump caught up with Cindy and the Birdman.

"What's this about a robbery at the museum?" asked Cal Crump.

Dexter glanced at the Birdman. The Birdman was looking at the bread in his cart. Dexter couldn't read his expression.

Just then a police car drove toward them, on the other side of the street. The policeman leaned out of the car window. Jay saw it was Hap Brady, the policeman he had met at the Coopers.

"Hey! Wait a minute," called Hap Brady. He turned the police car into a driveway, backed around, and pulled up next to the waiting group.

"Well, whaddya know, it's the cops!" said Cal Crump. "Rat-a-tat-tat! Duck, everyone!"

"Hello," said Hap Brady, getting out of the police car and walking over.

"Hello, Officer Brady," said Jay. "Remember me? You asked me to keep my eyes open. These are the other members of our detective club. And this is Cal Crump. His house was robbed, too. And this is . . ."

"Oh, you don't need to introduce me to the Birdman," laughed Hap Brady, clapping the Birdman on the back.

The Birdman smiled and nodded.

"Just stopped by to buy a loaf of bread. He's my walking bakery. Saves me a trip."

"I thought you were out investigating the robbery at the museum," said Jay.

"Museum robbery?" asked Hap Brady. "What do you mean?"

"Just a few minutes ago," said Dexter. "We reported it. The guard was going to call the police."

Hap Brady frowned. "Sounds like another petty theft by the sneak thief," he said.

"Nothing petty about a museum robbery," said

Cal Crump, frowning. "Museum stuff is pretty big business."

"I'll look into it now," said Hap Brady. "I'll just take along my loaf of bread, okay?" he asked. "My wife is going to make French toast again."

He reached into the cart for a loaf of bread and handed the Birdman some money.

"Here, take this one, Hap," said the Birdman quickly. "It's fresher."

"Oh, it's only for French toast," said Hap Brady. "It's really better if she starts out with stale bread."

He started back to his car.

"Bertha makes French toast, too," said Cal Crump. "Too fattening for me. And for her, if you want to know the truth, the whole truth, and nothing but the truth."

As Hap Brady started to get into the police car, a small object fell out of the bread bag. The policeman stopped and looked down.

"I'll get it," said Dexter, and ran to pick it up.

He stopped short as he leaned down. It was one

of the missing jade chessmen! He recognized it right away.

"It's the knight!" said Dexter hoarsely. "It's from the museum!"

Everyone froze. Everyone stared. First at Dexter holding the knight aloft, and then at the Birdman.

5 · It Can't Be!

HAP BRADY STOPPED in his tracks. Then he walked slowly back to the Birdman.

"Do you ever carry things in those paper bags— anything besides bread?" he asked, looking hard at the Birdman.

"No, I don't," said the Birdman, looking at his cart and frowning. "I don't know how that got there. I never saw it before. What is it, anyway? Some kind of toy?"

Hap Brady turned to Dexter. "Are you sure that this was stolen from the museum?"

Dexter looked at Jay. Jay nodded. Cindy stared miserably at her feet.

"I just don't know how it got there," the Birdman said again. "It must have—have fallen in. Or something like that."

He looked around and saw Cindy looking at him. "You believe me, don't you?" he asked. Cindy blinked and nodded.

"There's Agnes Lampkins, across the street," said Cindy suddenly. "Ask her, Officer Brady. She was very strange about the whole thing. Besides, she'd know for sure whether it is from the museum. She works there."

Hap Brady turned to Jay. "Ask her to come over a moment, if you will," he said. "Perhaps she can help us."

Jay ran across the street to Agnes Lampkins, who was shuffling along in her sloppy sneakers and swinging her purse. She saw Jay coming and stopped.

"Could you please come and talk to the policeman over there?" asked Jay. "It's about the stolen chess pieces."

"What do you mean, stolen? You mean missing. There's a heap of difference. How did *he* find out about it?" she asked angrily.

Jay glanced at her. Why was she angry—and surprised—that the police knew? She had said she was going to report the missing pieces, but she hadn't. Why not?

"Nothing but trouble with you kids," she said, glaring across the street. "You did the taking, and now you're trying to get everyone else in trouble. Kids like you should be locked up."

"We did not take anything," said Jay crossly. "But we did report it. The policeman wants to talk to you about the chess piece we've found over there. He wants you to identify it."

She smiled, suddenly and without gladness. "A chess piece has been found, eh? Think of that."

She followed Jay across the street.

"Good afternoon, madam," said Hap Brady. "I wonder if you have ever seen this object before?"

Agnes Lampkins looked at the chess piece. "I've seen it. I've seen it and seen it. And I don't care if I ever see it again. I've seen it a million times when I worked for Mr. Thorndyke. He always watched over his chess pieces. He didn't trust anyone. He didn't even trust me. It's hard to work for a man who doesn't trust people." She sniffed and peered around at the waiting group.

"You didn't report it was missing to anyone after all, did you?" blurted Jay.

Agnes Lampkins looked at Hap Brady and then back at Jay.

"Well, did you?" persisted Jay.

Agnes Lampkins glared at him. "No, I didn't, since you want to know."

"And why not, madam?" asked Hap Brady.

She paused a moment before answering.

"Because it's nobody's business, that's why. Nobody's business but Mr. Thorndyke's. There's one thing he has always hated, and that's people nosing around, knowing things. He hates publicity. And police . . . He would have handled this his own way. And now, these meddling kids had to spoil it all."

"A theft from a museum is the business of the police," said Hap Brady. "An individual can't handle something like that, and shouldn't. If I may just have your name and address and telephone number, I'd like to ask you some more questions later."

Agnes Lampkins hesitated. "I have no telephone," she said. "You can call me at the museum."

She started across the street, then looked back at Jay. "Two things I've always hated," she muttered. "Kids and police. They're always snooping."

She crossed the street and walked on, swinging her purse.

"It *is* funny that she promised she would report it and then didn't," said Cindy.

"Hmm," said Hap Brady.

"I'd like to go down to the police station," said the Birdman suddenly. "I want to make a statement."

Everyone stared at him.

"Make a statement!" echoed Cindy.

"I want to clear my name," he explained. "I want to prove I didn't take this thing. Or anything else. I've never even seen a chess set in my life."

"All right," said Hap Brady. "Let's just go down for a couple of questions and answers. No time like now."

"You're not going to arrest him, are you?" asked Cindy.

"Oh, no," said the policeman. "This is only routine. I'll want to ask you kids some questions, too, after I sort things out in my mind a little." He looked at his notebook. "If you'll just give me your names and telephone numbers," he said, "I can get in touch with you later."

"You don't think *we* had anything to do with it, do you?" asked Dexter, pushing his glasses up on his forehead.

"No, I don't," said Hap Brady. "But of course there may be some questions. You were right there, and you had just as much chance as Agnes Lampkins or the Birdman or Mr. Crump. Or anyone else. You were there."

"So were a million other people," sputtered Jay.

Cal Crump put his hands up. "Take me, I surrender, don't shoot," he laughed.

58

Hap Brady smiled. "They may regard the whole thing as a prank down at headquarters," he said. "We'll see."

Cindy stared at the policeman. "You're not serious that anyone could even think it was any of us?"

"We reported it," said Jay. "If we had taken anything, why would we have reported it?"

"Oh, as part of the prank, throwing suspicion on someone else," said Hap Brady. "Mind you, I don't believe that. But I'm just saying that some of the men down at the department who don't know you might wonder."

"I'm quite sure these children had nothing to do with it," said Cal Crump.

"They couldn't have had anything to do with anything," said the Birdman.

Hap Brady smiled and turned to the Birdman. "Shall we go?"

The Birdman nodded. "I just don't understand it," he said. "I just don't know how it got there, whatever it is."

"Can we do anything?" Cindy asked the Birdman.

The Birdman turned and smiled at her. "Yes, if you could take my cart. I don't live far from here. The little apartment building over on Elm Street. It's called Elmview. There's a little courtyard in front where I feed the birds. You might give them a little something. They'll be expecting me."

"Where will we leave the cart?" asked Jay.

"I have a storage space in the utility room, there at the back," said the Birdman. "Mine is locker Number 6. Here's the key, in case it's locked. I usually don't lock it, but I'm absentminded." He handed the key to Cindy.

"How can we get the key back to you?" asked Cindy.

"Oh, I'll be around," said the Birdman. "No hurry. Besides, I have lots of keys. In case I lose one, see?"

He looked at each of the children in turn. "Thanks. See you later." He walked slowly over to the police car and climbed in.

60

"It does look bad for the Birdman," Jay said as they watched the police car drive off.

"It doesn't look good, if you know what I mean," said Cal Crump. "Maybe your Breadman has crumbs where his brains should be."

"Birdman," said Cindy. "And no one has proved a thing yet."

"Birdman," said Cal Crump. "Then maybe he has feathers in his head." He laughed.

Cindy felt her throat tighten. "I don't know about the rest of you," she said, "but I'm going to try to prove he didn't do it."

"I agree with you, young lady," said Cal Crump, making a little bow to Cindy. "A man isn't guilty until he's proved guilty. But there are some interesting questions. Questions without answers. Why did he try to get the policeman to take a different loaf? How did the chess piece get into his bread bag? Ah well, you detectives will find out the answers to everything."

"Let's take his cart over to the Elmview and leave it," said Dexter. "Then we can sit down and figure out what clues we do have."

"I'll walk part way with you, if that's all right," said Cal Crump. "Give my bike a rest and my feet some exercise. Let my feet do the walking and my head do the talking."

62

Cindy and Dexter followed Jay and Cal Crump, who walked his bike.

"Do you realize what this means, Cindy?" asked Dexter, pushing his glasses up on his forehead. "If the Birdman took the chess pieces, then he probably is the one who's been doing all the little robberies in town." He shook his head. "He just doesn't seem like a bad guy. I'd rather believe Agnes Lampkins did it."

"I'm sure she did," said Cindy positively.

"Remember Mr. Hooley's rule," warned Dexter.

"Mr. Hooley's rule, Mr. Hooley's rule," said Cal Crump, looking back at them. "Who is Mr. Hooley and what is his rule?"

Dexter laughed. "We made it up. It just means you have to prove something."

"But what does this Hooley have to do with it?" said Cal Crump.

"We pretended a million dollars was stolen, and that it was discovered in a Mr. Hooley's basement. That doesn't prove that Mr. Hooley stole it. Someone else could have stolen it and hidden it in

Mr. Hooley's basement. Anyway, we call it Mr. Hooley's rule: You just can't guess at something. You have to prove it."

Cal Crump laughed. "Mr. Hooley's rule. Mr. Rooley's hool. Mr. Hooley's in hot water, I'd say, if that million dollars is in his basement. But it's a good rule. We can't jump to conclusions. It's too much exercise."

The children all laughed.

"And there are other rules, too," said Dexter, looking at Cindy. "Such as trying to solve a mystery even when you like the people you think might be guilty."

"All right, all right," said Cindy. "Let's find his apartment. Leave the bread for the birds. And then let's put his cart in his locker, okay? I want to figure it all out just as much as the rest of you."

As they neared the corner, the dog Randy ran up to them, wagging his tail. Then suddenly he stopped and growled.

"Hey, Randy," said Jay. "It's only us. What's wrong?"

Randy backed up, still growling. He put his tail between his legs.

"Guess he doesn't remember you, Cal, even with the bones you've been saving for him," said Jay.

"But he's always so friendly. Funny," said Dexter.

"Is he growling at me or at the Birdman's shopping cart?" asked Cal Crump. "Ah, well, wait till he sees the juicy bones I've saved. He'll sing a different tune then. Or bark a different bark." He laughed. Then he hopped on his bike. "I'll be going along. Keep me posted. Don't look so sad, young lady," he said to Cindy. "Your Birdman will be flying out of the police station in a short time."

"Thanks, I hope so," said Cindy.

Cal Crump waved and cycled down the street.

"Let's get on to the Elmview," Cindy said. "And then let's sit down and make our list of suspects— and clues. We've got plenty of both."

"The sooner we start, the sooner we'll get it solved," said Jay.

6 · *Too Many Suspects*

JAY, DEXTER, AND CINDY hurried their steps. In a few minutes they found the Elmview Apartments.

"But there aren't any elms left to view," said Dexter.

"Let's leave some bread for the birds, the way we promised," said Cindy.

"Hey, wait a minute," said Jay, turning to the cart. "Did we remember to tell Hap Brady two chess pieces were missing? Not just the one?"

"I don't think we did," said Dexter, pushing his glasses down on his nose.

66

"Maybe we should check all the bread bags," said Jay. "In all the excitement, I guess we did forget to say anything about there being two pieces stolen. Agnes Lampkins didn't say anything about it, either, come to think of it. If one was here in the cart, the other one might be, too."

"All right, go ahead. Look at the other loaves," said Cindy, pushing the cart over to Dexter. "I hope you don't find anything."

Dexter picked up each loaf and shook the bag. He looked in each. "Nothing," he said.

"Thank heaven," said Cindy.

"What kind of a detective are you?" asked Jay. "We're trying to find stolen property, and you're glad when we don't!"

"I just don't think we should jump to conclusions," said Cindy. "Remember Mr. Hooley's rule."

"Well, let's think up a rule that says you have to do everything you can to solve a mystery even if you think someone really nice is the bad guy," said Jay.

"Okay, let's think of that later," said Cindy.

"Now let's leave this cart where it belongs."

They walked around to the back of the building and found the utility room. They pushed the cart in and went to the storage compartment marked Locker 6.

"It is locked," said Jay. "Lucky he gave us a key." He turned the key the Birdman had given Cindy and walked in. Cindy followed him. Dexter pushed the cart.

There were many shelves in the dark locker, all of them crowded. The edge of the shopping cart caught on the edge of a soft, bulky package and pulled it off the shelf.

"Nothing broken," said Dexter, leaning over to pick it up. "It feels like a bundle of clothes or rags."

He started to push it back on the shelf. "Oops, I guess it goes the other way," he said. He stopped and peered on the shelf. "I guess I pushed when I should have pulled. I knocked something over. There must have been a box hidden back there. Lots of things spilled out."

"Oh, here, I'll pick up," said Cindy. She reached over to pick up the things that had spilled from the shelf.

They were chessmen.

Chessmen?

And the Birdman had said he'd never seen a chess set in his life!

Cindy slowly put the chess pieces back into the box where they had been. It was a brown carved box. No one would ever have seen it, hidden back there behind the bundle of clothing. A hidden box of chessmen!

"It's time to get mo-o-o-ving," said Dexter.

Cindy quickly wondered whether she should tell the boys about the chessmen. Then just as quickly she decided she would have to. The Spotlight Club had to work together. All for one, one for all, or it wasn't a club.

She walked out of the storage locker to where Jay and Dexter waited in the big utility room.

"The box hidden in there had chessmen in it. They were spilled out on the floor. I put them back," she said.

"A hidden box? Chessmen?" asked Jay. "But I thought the Birdman said . . ."

"I know, I know," said Cindy. "But remember Mr. Hooley's rule. We have to prove he did it." She pushed the hair out of her eyes. "Let's go on home and make a list of our clues and our other suspects. Agnes Lampkins, for instance."

"Yes," said Dexter. "She could have done it. And then put the chess piece in the Birdman's cart to make the blame fall on the Birdman."

"But how would she have known the policeman would come up and buy a loaf of bread?" asked Jay.

"Maybe the policeman did it," said Cindy. "Come on, let's hurry."

They started walking quickly back to the Temple house, their thoughts racing.

In a few minutes they were sitting around the kitchen table at the Temples with a plate of cookies in front of them. Cindy had a pad of paper and a pencil.

"All right, now," said Dexter. "First, let's see what proof we have against the Birdman. Then let's see what proof we have against anyone else."

"Don't leave anything out just because you like the Birdman, Cindy," said Jay.

"I won't," said Cindy. "But we've got to spend just as much time thinking of all the other suspects. It's only fair."

"Let's start with the most important clue," said Jay. "The chess piece was in the bag with the loaf of bread."

"I'm writing that down," said Cindy, "and I'm writing down right under it that someone else could have put it there."

"Okay," said Dexter. "Another thing is that the Birdman was in the museum at the time the chess pieces were stolen. Remember he had to get a drink of water. And the drinking fountain is right next to the chess set."

"And the third thing is that he seemed upset when he came out," said Jay.

"He was upset because Agnes Lampkins yelled at him," said Cindy. "I'm putting that down, too."

"Then I saw the Birdman putting something in the fountain," said Dexter.

Cindy wrote. "I put that down. And I also put down that everyone drops pennies in the fountain."

"What else?" asked Jay, tapping his head. "There was something else. Oh, Anne saw the Birdman at Random Park when Sally's car was robbed."

"That isn't fair," said Cindy. "She didn't see him necessarily. She saw *someone* feeding birds. And even if he was there, that doesn't mean a thing. Lots of people were there."

"Yes, but we have so many reasons for suspecting him already," said Jay. "And we haven't any reason to suspect all the other people at Random Park."

"That's no reason to be careless with our clues," said Cindy.

"Okay, okay," said Jay. "But we do have one other big thing against the Birdman. He lied about not knowing anything about chess. He said he'd never even seen a chess set. And he had one hidden in his locker."

"That's right, Cindy," Dexter said.

"I'm putting that down," said Cindy. "And now let's have a list for Agnes Lampkins. That will be more fun."

"Well," said Dexter, "Agnes Lampkins does act guilty. She could be Mr. X."

"Miss X," said Cindy. "A sneak thief-ess."

"She had a chance to take the chess pieces, all right," said Dexter. "She was right there. And she knows they are valuable. She might have been planning to take them all and put them in that big purse. Then we came in to get a drink of water and we stopped her."

"Yes," said Cindy excitedly, "and she was all ready to leave, and the museum was closing. She thought no one would be coming back in."

"She thought it wouldn't be discovered until the next day. So she would have had plenty of chance to hide the chessmen. Then she got worried when we came in and discovered they were missing. She had to hurry and hide them. So she hid one in the Birdman's cart as she was leaving the museum park."

"And she lied to us, saying she was going to report it. She just didn't want us to report it," said Jay.

"But she was afraid we would, so she had to get rid of the evidence," said Cindy. "I'm writing all of it down."

The back door opened and Mrs. Temple walked in, carrying her coat. "Aha, snack thieves," she said, seeing the cookies.

"They're great, Mom," said Cindy.

"You can eat the whole house if you like, as long as you're working on those museum reports for school. And I can see you are," said Mrs. Temple, as she glanced at the paper on the table and the notes.

Jay shuffled through the papers. "Well, sure, Mom, we're going to get those done in time for school tomorrow. But right now we've got something much more important."

"Yes, a real mystery, Mrs. Temple," said Dexter.

"The real mystery will be how you can pass Social Studies if you don't settle down and do those papers," said Mrs. Temple, opening the refrigerator.

"Tonight, Mom, honest," said Jay.

"Yes, and we'll all get A's,"said Cindy. "Mom, we went to the museum, and some chess pieces were stolen—we were right there."

"Really?" asked Mrs. Temple, turning around.

They told her all about the afternoon. "It's funny, isn't it, Mrs. Temple?" said Dexter. "A conch shell, a pepper mill, some old tennis balls, a couple of chessmen—I don't understand. I don't understand what Mr. X could do with things like that. Or why he'd want them."

"Maybe he's a kleptomaniac," suggested Mrs. Temple, sitting at the table with the children.

"A what-so-maniac?" asked Cindy.

"Kleptomaniac," said Mrs. Temple.

"Someone who sets fires?" asked Dexter.

"No, that's a pyromaniac," said Mrs. Temple. "A kleptomaniac takes things. He has an urge to steal. Even if he has no use for what he steals, he takes things anyway. He can't help it. Maybe he already has a dozen—oh, let's say a dozen rulers, for instance. A whole box of rulers. That doesn't keep him from taking more rulers. For a kleptomaniac, stealing is like hiccups. He can't stop it. It's a sickness."

"I hope it isn't catching, like a cold," said Dexter.

"You'd all better write your papers before you catch something else," she laughed. "I really mean it."

"My paper route!" said Jay, suddenly. "I forgot!"

"Why don't you see if Travis Hackworthy can do it?" asked Dexter.

"Good idea," said Jay, running into the hall to the telephone. In a moment he was back. "Good old Trav. He'll take it today and tomorrow. That means I'm free as a bird to work on the mystery."

"To work on your paper, you mean," said Mrs. Temple. "First things first. What did you decide to write on?"

Jay thought quickly. "Bicycles," he said. "The old-fashioned kind, and then the new ten-speed kind like the one Cal Crump has."

"I was going to do one on dolls, rag dolls, and those new talking dolls. But now I'm going to do it on the loom, I think. People used to make their own materials," Cindy said.

"How about you, Dexter?" asked Mrs. Temple. "What will you write about?"

"I was thinking about those old muskets. Then I thought maybe the oil lamps, compared to electric lights today."

Mrs. Temple stood up. "Why don't you do your papers right now? Dexter, you can stay for supper if you like, and you can all work together."

"I'd love to, Mrs. Temple," said Dexter. "I'll call Mom."

"All right, gang," said Cindy. "Let's get the papers over with."

"Be sure to put the encyclopedias back when you're through," said Mrs. Temple. "Last time you left them all over the place."

By seven o'clock the detectives had finished their papers, had supper, and were working again on the list of suspects.

"Where were we?" asked Dexter.

"We had the Birdman and Agnes Lampkins," said Cindy, looking at her notes. "Agnes Lampkins might have taken those chessmen because she was mad at Mr. Thorndyke. And I thought of something else fishy about her. Remember she said Mr. Thorndyke didn't trust anybody? Well, maybe he didn't trust her because he knew she was a pyromaniac."

"Klepto," said Jay. "Kleptomaniac."

"Hey—I've got it!" said Dexter. "I've got it, I've got it, I've got it."

"Maybe it is catching," said Cindy, laughing.

"No, seriously, listen," said Dexter. "That workman, remember? What was his name?"

"Grubbs," said Cindy.

"That's it, Mr. Grubbs. Remember he said the park had to be closed right away because the museum director had said so?"

Jay and Cindy thought a moment. "Yes," said Jay. "I remember."

"I think I do, too," said Cindy. "What about it?"

"Well, when we told the guard about the robbery, he said the director was gone for the day." Dexter looked at their surprised faces.

"Mr. Grubbs lied—but why?" asked Cindy.

"To get everyone out so he could steal the chess pieces," said Dexter. "Then Agnes Lampkins spoiled it all for him by appearing when he hadn't expected her."

"Yes, and he could have planted that one chess piece in the Birdman's cart when he'd been discovered!" said Cindy. "That proves . . ."

"Proves nothing," said Dexter. "Remember Mr. Hooley's rule."

Cindy held up her notes. "So far we have Agnes Lampkins, the Birdman, and Mr. Grubbs."

"And any one of them could be Mr. X," said Dexter. "And what about Cal Crump?" asked Dexter. "He was in the museum, too."

"Right, he was," said Jay. "And so let's put him down. And let's put down . . ."

Dexter jumped up. "Why are we sitting around? Why don't we go over to the museum park right now and look in the fountain? If the chess piece is there, it proves that it was the Birdman. I saw him put something in."

"Well, someone else could have put it there," said Cindy. "But I'd rather find out for sure anyway. The suspense is killing me."

"The museum park is locked," said Jay. "That means no one could have gone in to remove the evidence."

"And how will we get in?" asked Cindy.

"Climb the fence," said Dexter.

"Let's go," said Jay. "Bye, Mom!" he called up the stairs.

"Where are you going?" called Mrs. Temple. "It's dark."

"We'll be right back," promised Cindy.

"All right, but if you're not back by the time my hair is dry I'll start to worry," said Mrs. Temple.

The three detectives ran down the steps.

7 · Chase in the Dark

WHEN DEXTER, Jay, and Cindy arrived at the museum park, they were out of breath. "The lowest part of the fence is the part near the gate," whispered Cindy.

Jay held his flashlight. He shone it around the gate.

"Look," he whispered. "The gate's open!"

Dexter pulled his glasses down on his nose and leaned over. "Someone's unlocked it," he whispered.

"Or else someone left it open by mistake," said Cindy.

"I doubt it," said Dexter, trying to keep his voice down. "Museum park gates aren't left open by mistake. Someone opened it. Either with the museum key or with a skeleton key."

"And whoever opened it must be in there now," said Jay.

Cindy shivered. "I'm scared," she said.

"You can wait out here," Dexter whispered.

"Not me," said Cindy bravely, "I'm going in if you are. But you go first."

The three slid noiselessly through the gate and stood silently, listening. Jay had turned off his flashlight. There was no sound. Dexter pulled at Jay's sleeve and motioned to the fountain. They tiptoed quietly over the grass.

Suddenly Cindy saw a shape. It loomed out of the darkness. She held back a scream and grabbed Jay. She pointed to the big shadowy shape. It was very still, only a few yards away.

Cindy felt Jay stiffen, then relax. "It's just a statue," he whispered. "Come on. I don't think anyone else is around. Whoever was here probably climbed over the fence and ran off when he heard us coming."

The three tiptoed across the grass toward the fountain.

"Be careful of the new cement," Jay warned.

Dexter whispered to Jay and Cindy, "I know just where the Birdman was standing when he leaned over and dropped something in the fountain. I'll reach in. You shine the light, Jay."

Dexter walked over to the fountain and pointed. "Right around there," he said. "This is just where he was standing. Then he leaned down like this . . ."

Jay shone the flashlight on the water. The coins in the fountain glittered.

Suddenly Dexter whispered, "There it is! I see it! I was right!" Jay leaned over to see better.

Cindy looked nervously around. Her heart beat fast as she glimpsed a dark shape. Then she remembered it was just a statue.

But—the statue moved closer. It raised an arm.

Cindy screamed. "Run!" she shouted.

Dexter lost his balance and fell into the water.

"What's wrong with you?" asked Jay. He was angry.

"Someone's coming!" Cindy cried.

Jay turned and caught a glimpse of the big shadowy figure coming toward them, waving its arms.

Dexter was sputtering in the water. He splashed around in the fountain, trying to get to his feet. "My glasses," he said, groping around.

"Never mind the glasses," shouted Jay. "Hurry! Run for your life!"

He helped Dexter out of the water. "We'll climb the fence and get away," Jay said. "This way—toward the pond."

Jay ran, then stumbled and fell. He struggled to his feet. Then he felt himself being pushed down. Someone had run up behind him. Someone strong. Someone big. It was too dark, and it all happened too fast for Jay to see anything.

By the time Jay got to his feet, no one was in sight. And Dexter and Cindy were gone. Had someone knocked them down, too?

"Dexter! Cindy!" Jay called. "Are you okay?"

He forgot about the wet cement around the fountain. Ooops! Running, he put one foot down in the new cement. For a second he thought he was in trouble for sure. With a tug he freed his foot and ran, not looking back.

"Over here, quick," shouted Dexter.

Jay ran toward Dexter's voice, over near the fence. "Here's a place we can climb. Cindy, we'll boost you over."

"Boost, nothing," said Cindy. "I'm already up."

At last! The three were safely on the other side of the fence. They stood and listened. There was no sound but the beating of their hearts.

"That was close," said Dexter, panting.

Then they heard footsteps running down the sidewalk, running away from them. They listened. The footsteps went farther and farther away.

"He's gone! We scared him off!" said Jay.

"Who scared *who* off?" said Cindy. "I just lost a year of my life."

"I've got to go back in and get my glasses. And

that chess piece," said Dexter. "I know I saw it."

"Forget the glasses," said Cindy. "We can lead you around. And that chess piece, how about getting it early in the morning? Daylight and all that?"

"No, we've got to go back in now. You can wait outside, Cindy," said Jay.

"Big deal," said Cindy. "Mr. X is on the outside now, remember? I'll go in with you."

"If the chess piece is in there, he'll come back for it after we go," said Dexter. "We've got to get it now. But I don't know how I'll find it without my glasses."

"Find your glasses first," said Cindy.

"I can't find my glasses without my glasses," said Dexter.

"Come on," said Jay. "But this time let's go through the gate."

They walked down to the gate, stopping and listening every few steps. There was no sound.

"It's locked!" said Jay, trying the gate. "He locked it when he left."

"Then it's up and over again," said Cindy.

"Twice. Let's get it over with. This time I'll need a boost."

Jay found Dexter's glasses in the fountain. Dexter took the flashlight and looked for the chess piece.

"It's gone," he said finally. "He got it!"

"That's why he pushed me down," said Jay. "So he would have time to run back to the fountain and get it."

"That proves it couldn't have been the Birdman," said Cindy. "He wouldn't push anyone."

"No?" asked Jay.

"No," said Cindy.

"But then what *did* he put in the fountain? And did he come back for it?" asked Jay. "There's something fishy here."

"A goldfish," said Cindy.

There was a sudden whirring sound. Cindy screamed. A big white shape rose out of the darkness. It headed straight for Cindy. She ducked behind Jay.

"Grab him! Hit him!" she screamed. Jay fell over, and Dexter tripped on Jay's legs.

While they were trying to get untangled, Cindy looked fearfully around. Then she started to laugh.

"It's only a swan," she said. "Go away, Albert! Or Einstein! Or Rose! Or Thorn!" she called. "Go away!"

Jay picked himself up. "Let's get out of here," he said.

"Yes, sir!" said Cindy. "On the double."

"I'll buy that," said Dexter.

They climbed the fence. "Let's come back early in the morning, the way Cindy said," suggested Jay. "Maybe we can find out who was here tonight."

The Spotlight Club members walked slowly home, looking at each doorway. Someone might be waiting in the shadows.

"Who would have a key?" asked Dexter, and then said, "Mr. Grubbs!"

"And maybe Agnes Lampkins," said Jay. "Look at the cement on my shoe. I'll have to clean it off right away."

"Let's see what happens tomorrow morning," said Cindy. "I'm all scared out for one night."

90

8 · Shoes and Clues

EARLY NEXT MORNING, the three Spotlighters cycled to the museum, prepared to climb the fence.

"Glad my bike's fixed, finally," said Jay on the way over. "I'm going to start saving for a ten-speeder, like the one Cal Crump has."

"You'll be as old as he is by the time you save up that much," said Dexter.

When they got to the museum, the three found to their surprise that the gate was standing open.

They pushed their bikes in and stared.

Mr. Grubbs was standing near the fountain

and frowning. He turned around when he heard them.

Then he looked back at the fountain. Frowning even more, he walked quickly over to them.

"Okay!" he shouted angrily. "I knew I was going to have more trouble with you. This is the end. You kids stay out of here from now on. Climbing the fence at night, eh? We'll have to put spikes on the fence next!"

Jay swallowed. "How did you know we were in here last night?" he asked. "How did you know—unless you saw us here last night?"

"And how did you know we climbed the fence?" asked Dexter.

The three stared at Mr. Grubbs.

"How did you know—unless you were in here, too?" asked Cindy.

Mr. Grubbs reddened. "And what would I be doing in the park at night, eh? And if I were in the park at night, what business would it be of yours?" He pointed at the gate. "Now you just turn around and march out of here before I tell the director."

"The director!" said Cindy. "You said you'd talked to him yesterday. You said he told you to close the museum early, and the park, too."

"Yeah, so what about it?" asked Mr. Grubbs.

"He wasn't in. The director was gone all day!" said Cindy triumphantly.

Mr. Grubbs seemed to be taken aback. "Nosey, aren't you?" he demanded. "Well, you can just nose your way out of here, right now! The park won't be open until nine o'clock. And if I see you here then, I'll report you to the truant officer!"

"We're not going. Yet," said Jay, bravely. "Not until we know how you knew we were in here last night."

"Smart-aleck, aren't you?" asked Mr. Grubbs. "Maybe too smart for your own good!"

A workman who was laying sod down near the pond whistled and motioned to Mr. Grubbs. Mr. Grubbs nodded to the man. Then he turned to Jay. "I have more work to do, thanks to your meddling! See that you're out of here—but fast!"

He turned and stalked off down the slope to the pond.

"That proves he was here, and that proves he was the one," said Cindy excitedly. "I bet he came back for the chess piece."

"It looks that way," said Dexter, staring thoughtfully at Mr. Grubbs as he strode down the slope. "But we have to be positive. Mr. Hooley's rule, remember?"

"Why did he want us out of here so fast?" puzzled Jay. "Maybe so he could cover his tracks from last night."

Dexter snapped his fingers. "The fountain. He was looking at it when we came, remember? He seemed upset when we saw him!"

Dexter ran over to the fountain, the others at his heels. "Look," he whispered.

There in the new cement on one side were two footprints. "Look at that," said Jay.

One was a smaller footprint that was smudged. Jay's. The other was a very big print. Much too big to belong to one of the Spotlight Club members.

"The cement they poured yesterday was still soft last night," said Cindy. "That smaller footprint must be yours, Jay. And the big one . . ." she pointed to Mr. Grubbs, who was deep in conversation with the workman. "He wanted to get us out of here before we could see that track. And check it with his shoes," she said.

"Proof! We've got proof. In hard cement," said Jay.

"Not until we can prove this footprint was made by Mr. Grubbs," said Dexter. "All we have to do is match this print with one of Mr. Grubbs's. Because whoever was in here last night left this print. And whoever left this print took the chess piece."

"Mr. X," said Cindy. "But how are we going to get a look at his shoes?" asked Jay. "He won't let us within a mile of him. And now he'll know we saw the print in the cement. He must have just seen it when he came in to work this morning.

"No wonder he was upset," said Dexter. "He had to remove the evidence before we saw it."

At that moment the Spotlighters heard Agnes Lampkins's shrill voice. "Hey, what are you doing there? Get away from that fountain." She ran down the steps toward them.

"We're just looking," said Cindy.

"You've caused enough mischief around here to last all year," she said. "Now you get out of here this minute! It's bad enough you were here sneaking around last night."

The three detectives exchanged glances.

"Out you go," she said. "Quick!"

They walked over to their bikes and pushed them through the gate.

As soon as the three were outside, Cindy whispered, "She knew we were here, too. And did you see her feet? She wasn't wearing those big old sloppy sneakers. She was wearing black shoes! Maybe it was her footprint in the cement. She certainly wanted us out of there before we'd have a chance to look."

They hurried to school. "It's going to be one long day," said Cindy. "The mystery nearly solved, and us stuck in school!"

"Tell you what," said Jay. "Right after school let's dump our books at home and find the Birdman."

"Mr. X is either Agnes Lampkins or Mr. Grubbs," said Cindy. "Why do you want to prove the Birdman is guilty?"

"I don't," said Jay. "I'm trying to prove him innocent. If he can prove he was somewhere else last night, that he couldn't have been in the park, then we know for sure he's innocent."

"Oh, good," said Cindy. "Then I want to find him. A good detective has to prove people innocent. That's as important as proving the real one guilty."

"We're getting closer and closer to the real Mr. X," said Jay.

"Or Miss X," said Cindy.

9 · Closing In

AFTER SCHOOL, the Spotlighters sped home on their bikes. "Let's leave our books. And our bikes," said Dexter. "Yours is falling apart again, Jay."

As they ran out the front door, Jay saw a couple of folded pages of a magazine on the porch. "Wait, I'll just throw these out," he said, crumpling them up. "You know how Mom hates to have trash blow up on the porch."

"Oh, come on," said Cindy. "We'll get it when we get back. Let's go to see the Birdman. I've got to know he's innocent."

Jay stuffed the wadded paper in his pocket

and ran down the porch steps with Dexter and Cindy.

They were just turning the corner to Elm Street when they heard a horn honking. It was Hap Brady. They ran over to him.

"Have we got a lot to tell you!" said Jay.

"There were two chessmen stolen!" Dexter said. "We forgot to tell you about that before."

"I know about it. One of the museum guards reported it," said Hap Brady.

"Agnes Lampkins?" asked Cindy.

"No, the other guard," the policeman answered. "But here's a puzzling new mystery," he said, handing something to Jay. "I really shouldn't be showing you this," he said. "You're still on the suspect list, you know."

They stared at him.

Cindy gulped. "You mean *we're* suspects?"

Hap Brady nodded. "I guess you are. Not that I suspect you myself. I know good kids when I see them. And good detectives," he added, with a twinkle in his eyes. "That's why I want you to take a look at this."

Cindy and Dexter looked over Jay's shoulder as he turned the envelope over. The envelope was addressed to Mr. Thorndyke, the rich owner of the chess set.

Jay opened the envelope and took out a folded sheet of paper. Pasted on it were words cut from a magazine. Jay could tell because of the shiny paper.

Cindy and Dexter looked over Jay's shoulder as he read. The message said:

WANT YOUR JADE KING?

I NEED $

WAIT FOR A CALL

"A ransom note," breathed Cindy. "A ransom note for a chess piece. Mr. X—or Miss X—wants money. Money in exchange for the chessmen."

"Yes," said Hap Brady. "And if old Mr. Thorndyke had gotten this message, he probably would have paid the thief. He wouldn't have gone to the police. He would be afraid everything would get in the newspaper. He hates that kind of thing."

Cindy nodded. "That's what Agnes Lampkins said."

Dexter looked puzzled. "If the note was for Mr. Thorndyke, how did you get it?" he asked.

"Luck," laughed Officer Brady. "Mr. Thorndyke was so upset when he learned a chess piece was missing that he didn't sleep a wink last night. He was asleep this morning when the message came. His secretary opened it."

"But why is that lucky?" asked Jay.

"Because the secretary called us at the police station. That's how we got the note."

"And the thief's plans are spoiled," said Cindy slowly. "Whoever sent the note must have known Mr. Thorndyke wouldn't call the police."

They all looked at the ransom note again.

"Well, you kids can play detective for me, if you don't mind," said Hap Brady, as Jay handed the note back to him. "People will talk to kids when they clam up with a policeman. See what you can find out."

"We've found out a lot already," said Jay. "Last night—"

The Spotlighters told Officer Brady about their

scary adventure in the museum park.

"The person who stepped in the cement has to be the thief," Dexter said.

"And that person has to be Mr. Grubbs," said Cindy.

"Or Agnes Lampkins," said Dexter.

"Or the Birdman," said Jay.

"I'll tell you what," said Hap Brady. "Write it all down. Write down only the important things you find out. The things you are sure about. And drop the letter off at the station if I'm not around. A ransom note is serious business. We don't want to accuse anyone until we're absolutely sure."

"Mr. Hooley's rule," said Cindy.

"The law," said Hap Brady. "And good sense. And fair play, and all that."

"We're on our way to see the Birdman," said Cindy. "We want to prove he's innocent."

Hap Brady smiled. "I hope you can prove that," he said. "I've always liked him. But you know that doesn't prove a thing. Some of the most charming people I've ever met are crooks."

He started to drive away. "Let me know what you find out," he said.

The three detectives hurried on. "A ransom note. What next?" asked Dexter, pushing his glasses up on his forehead.

"Oh, come on," said Cindy.

They rounded the corner to Elm Street. Just ahead was the Birdman's apartment building, the Elmview. And just ahead was the Birdman. He was carrying a paper bag and walking toward the back of the building.

"Hello, Birdman," called Cindy.

The Birdman paused and looked around. He saw them. Then he looked down at the paper bag he was carrying.

"Oh, hello," he said. "Hello."

Cindy glanced down at the Birdman's shoes. His usual high walking boots with the laces had been replaced by shiny new black shoes.

He saw her glance. "I got my boots all muddy," he said. "I was just going to take them back and wash them off in the utility room." He seemed uneasy. "I have some chores to do this afternoon," he said. "I'm sorry I won't have time to visit with you."

"We just wanted to ask you something," said Cindy. "Where were you last night?" She blurted it out.

The Birdman looked up, frowning.

"Where was I last night? Why? Who wants to know? The police?" He looked again at the paper bag. "I wasn't anywhere," he said.

Dexter broke in. "We're just trying to prove something," he said.

"Prove what?" asked the Birdman. "Are you thinking it was me who took that thing from the museum?"

"No," said Cindy. "We just wanted to prove you didn't do it. We wanted to see if you had an alibi for last night."

The Birdman looked from one to the other. "Why, I was here at home," he said. Then he sighed. "No, I took a walk. Got my boots muddy."

"Can you prove where you were?" asked Cindy anxiously.

The Birdman shook his head. "I didn't see any-one. And no one saw me, either. It was dark." He looked at Cindy. "And I still don't know why it matters where I was. Nobody's ever bothered before, about me."

"Well, never mind," said Cindy. "We're just trying to put some pieces of the puzzle together."

"Let's go," said Jay. "We've still a few more stops to make."

They waved good-bye to the Birdman. Cindy looked back as they walked away. The Birdman was walking over to the trash cans. He lifted the lid of one and put the paper bag inside. Cindy frowned. He had said he was going to wash off his boots, not throw them away. Was one of them covered with cement? Should they wait until he had gone and then check the boots for any telltale signs of cement?

She walked behind the boys for a few steps. They were chattering away. Cindy took a deep breath. She'd have to tell them about the Birdman throwing the boots away. It probably didn't mean anything anyway. Or did it?

Just then Jay reached into his pockets. He drew something out in surprise. "What's this? Oh, the junk that was on our porch." He looked for a trash can.

"I was just looking back," said Cindy, "and— not that it means anything, but I happened to see—"

Jay stopped in his tracks. He was staring at the crumpled sheet in his hand.

"This paper was on our porch. Look!" he exclaimed. "It's full of little holes. Someone cut letters and words out of it."

"Let me see," Cindy said.

"Me, too," said Dexter, pulling his glasses down on his nose.

Jay smoothed the paper out. It was the cover from a magazine: *The Birdwatchers Journal.* Jay turned it over.

There was an advertisement for bird prints. Several words had been cut out.

Dexter pointed. "Look, somebody cut out the $-sign that went in front of the price."

The Spotlight Clubbers stared at each other. They were all thinking the same thing.

"The ransom note," Jay said. "This is the page Mr. X cut up for the ransom note!"

Cindy frowned. "How did it get on our porch?" she asked. "That's an awfully funny thing just to happen."

"Maybe the wind blew it there," Jay said.

"Let me see it," Dexter said. "Hey! Here's an address label pasted on the front cover: E. Z. Quayle, 455 Elm, Kenoska, Illinois."

Cindy's heart was pounding. "E. Z. Quayle," she moaned. "Oh, no."

The boys looked at her. "Who's E. Z. Quayle?" asked Jay.

Cindy gulped. "Ezra Zebediah Quayle," said Cindy. "The Birdman. He told me his real name."

The three stood and looked at the magazine cover. "I just can't believe it was the Birdman," said Cindy. "Sending a ransom note. Stealing the chess pieces."

"Yeah," said Jay. "I'd rather believe it was Agnes Lampkins or Mr. Grubbs. Or someone else we don't like."

"That's the trouble with being detectives," said Dexter. "But we wouldn't be much of a detective club if we decided ahead of time who was or wasn't guilty."

"I know," said Cindy sadly.

"We've got to see Hap Brady," said Jay. "We have to show him the magazine cover. It's a piece of evidence. It's important."

The three started to walk to the police station, each busy with his own thoughts.

"I think it is very, very fishy that the page with his name on it landed on our porch," said Cindy.

"What do you mean, fishy?" asked Jay.

"Funny. Strange. Peculiar. Odd," said Cindy. "One chance in a million. A coincidence. An important clue just happening to blow up on our porch. Just *happening* to. On *our* porch of all porches."

"Well, it was lucky," said Jay.

"Was it just luck, though?" asked Cindy. "Was it an accident? Or was it on purpose?"

Dexter scratched his head. "I see what you mean," he said. "It's almost as if it had just happened to blow right onto Hap Brady's desk."

"Well, we'll have to show it to him anyway," said Jay.

They walked along. "I still don't think the Birdman can be guilty," said Cindy.

"Remember our new rule," said Jay. "We can't let our feelings about anyone keep us from being good detectives."

"I know," said Cindy unhappily. "But we can't accuse the Birdman just because of one little thing. Just because he takes a subscription to a magazine, and the magazine has some holes..."

Her voice trailed off. It did look as if everything was pointing to the Birdman. The black knight in the bag of bread. The chess pieces in the hidden box. The boots in the trash can. And now this!

As they hurried along, they passed Cal Crump's house. He was doing deep knee bends on the front porch.

"What's new?" he called when he saw them. "How's the mystery? Any bullet wounds? Trails of blood? Found the murder weapon yet? Or the body? Ha, Ha!"

The door opened and Bertha Crump stepped out on the porch. She was holding Cal Crump's special bicycle shoes.

"Honestly, Cal," she said. "What on earth were you doing last night? It looks as if you stepped in cement. I can't get it off."

Cal Crump turned and stared at the shoes.

"Just a little mud, my dear. Here, I'll clean them up, nothing to it." He reached quickly for his shoes. "I'll just take them out to the garage. No problem." He put the shoes under his arm and turned to step off the porch. "Bertha's a nut about housekeeping. Wonderful woman. Every piece of dust looks like a mountain to Bertha. Right, Bertha, my dear?"

He winked at Jay. "I hope you are lucky enough to get a wife like my Bertha." He nodded at the three detectives. "See you around, as the hole said to the donut." He trotted back to the garage with the shoes. The Spotlighters stared after him.

Bertha Crump shook her head. "Men are just like children," she said. She held up a jacket. "He tore his jacket last night, too. And it's all dirty. I'll just send it to the cleaners. They'll mend it." She reached into the pocket of the jacket to empty it. "Why, what's this?" She held something up.

It was the missing chess piece.

10 · No Missing Pieces

JAY, CINDY, AND DEXTER stared at the chess piece. And then they stared at each other.

"The things that man keeps in his pockets," said Bertha Crump, laughing. "And in his closet! My goodness. When I was cleaning Cal's closet just now I found all kinds of things. They were stashed away in a box hidden under his sweaters. A beautiful conch shell, some old tennis balls, a pile of ashtrays. We don't smoke, you know. He doesn't believe in it. So what does he want with ashtrays?"

Mrs. Crump shook her head. "Men," she said. "They're just like little boys."

The three detectives felt their hearts pound. Jay was the first to speak. "We've got to be going," he said. "Say good-bye to Mr. Crump, to Cal, for us."

They almost ran down the porch steps. When the Crump house was out of sight, Dexter said, "I guess we found Mr. X just in time. We've got to get to Hap Brady in a hurry. Before Cal Crump hides the chess piece and the other things he stole."

They were at the police station in a few minutes. "We'd like to see Officer Brady, please," said Dexter. "It's important."

They ran over to the desk that was pointed out to them.

Hap Brady looked up in surprise.

"We've found the thief!" said Jay. "And the chess piece. And everything."

"But you'll have to hurry," said Cindy. "He's probably finding out right now that we know."

"He may hide the evidence!" said Dexter, pushing his glasses up.

"What? What are you talking about?" asked Hap Brady.

"It's Cal Crump," said Jay. "He's the thief."

"Cal Crump? The guy with the fancy bike?" Hap Brady stood up. "How do you know?"

"He has the chess piece. And he has a closet full of the stolen things," said Jay. "All hidden in an old box."

"Yes, and his shoe has cement on it," said Cindy. "We'll tell you that story later."

"Are you sure about all this?" asked Hap Brady.

"Positive!" said Dexter.

"I guess you really are detectives," said Hap Brady. "Okay, I'll take a drive over there now." He started out of the office. "I've got your telephone numbers. I'll call you tonight and let you know all about it."

They followed him, at a run, out of the office. They watched the police car back out of the driveway.

Then they turned to each other.

"We've solved it! We solved the mystery!" said Cindy.

"Let's tell Mom," said Jay.

"And Anne and my folks," said Dexter.

"And then the Birdman," said Cindy.

"Hey, we're heroes!" said Jay.

"You and Dexter are," said Cindy. "I'm a heroine."

They raced home. Mr. Tate was just driving into the driveway.

"Hey, Dad," called Dexter. "We've got news for you!"

"Just what I need," said Mr. Tate, grinning. "The evening newspaper, right?"

"We've solved the mystery, Mr. Tate," said Jay.

"What mystery?" asked Mr. Tate, getting out of the car.

"The mystery of the sneak thief and the mystery of the museum. We've already told the police," said Cindy.

"Wait a minute," said Mr. Tate, frowning. "You can't go running off to the police unless you're sure of your facts."

Anne walked out onto the porch. "What's this about police?" she asked.

"We'll tell you everything," said Dexter. "Where's Mom? We want her to hear, too."

"It sounds as if it's something we'll all want to hear about," said Mr. Tate. "Anne, ask Mother if that stew she's made will stretch a little. And Jay and Cindy, won't you ask your mother to come over? We'll have a lot to talk about tonight."

In a short time they were all sitting around the supper table: Mr. and Mrs. Tate, Anne, Mrs. Temple, and Jay, Cindy, and Dexter.

"It's a party!" said Cindy. "Candles and everything!"

"Now let's start at the beginning," said Mr. Tate. "All we've heard so far are bits and pieces, with everyone talking at once."

"Let's start at the end and do it backwards," said Jay.

"I can't talk backwards," said Cindy. "Especially when I'm eating."

"So let's eat first," laughed Mrs. Tate.

Just as they were finishing supper, the doorbell rang. It was Hap Brady.

"I just wanted to stop in to thank you three detectives for solving the mystery," he said when Dexter opened the door.

"Do sit down with us and have some coffee, Officer," said Mrs. Tate.

"Did Cal confess?" Dexter asked.

Hap Brady did most of the talking. "Well, I drove over to Cal Crump's house in the police car. He was sitting on the porch, holding the chess piece."

"You mean he hadn't tried to run away or hide the piece or anything?" asked Jay.

"No, he was sort of waiting for me," said Hap Brady. "His wife had told him about finding the chess piece. He knew you kids would guess he was the thief. He wanted to come over to headquarters to confess. He said it would make him feel better. He was tired of lying all the time."

"Just think," said Cindy, "it was Cal Crump all the time. We never really suspected him."

Hap Brady smiled. "After I took Cal to the police station, I went over to tell the Birdman that Cal had confessed. I didn't want the Birdman to worry anymore. And I stopped to see Mr. Grubbs and Agnes Lampkins. They cleared up some things, too. I think we have all the answers now."

"Do start at the beginning, Officer," said Anne. "Everything is whirling around in my head."

Hap Brady nodded. "Cal Crump stole the two pieces from the chess set that afternoon at the museum. He thought all along that Mr. Thorndyke wouldn't tell the police. And Cal thought he could get Mr. Thorndyke to pay to get his chess pieces back."

Dexter said, "And Mr. Thorndyke would have done that, but he never saw the ransom note. It was just lucky his secretary opened the mail that morning and called the police."

"Did Cal Crump do those other robberies, too?" asked Mr. Tate.

"All of them," said Hap Brady.

"But why?" asked Mrs. Temple.

"Because he wanted everyone to think that the thief was a—what's that word?" asked Dexter, looking at Jay.

"Klepto—kleptomaniac," said Jay.

"What's that?" asked Anne.

"Someone who just takes things to hide away in some hidden box. He doesn't need the things," explained Cindy.

"You see," said Hap Brady, "Cal was trying to throw everyone off the track. When the chess pieces were discovered missing, everyone would think it was just something else the sneak thief had taken."

"Then he was just building up to the theft of the chess pieces," said Dexter.

"That's right," said Hap Brady. "That way, no one would think the king and the knight had been stolen with any ransom or anything in mind. They'd just think it was another thing the kleptomaniac picked up on an impulse."

"Cal Crump was all over town on his bike. He could take something and be gone in a flash," said Jay. "It's quite a bike."

"At the museum, Cal thought no one would notice the pieces were missing until the next day because the museum was closing," said Hap Brady.

"When he heard you kids shouting about it, he knew the game was up. He was afraid everyone would be searched." Hap Brady paused.

"What did he do with the chess pieces?" asked Mrs. Temple.

"He just walked outside and carefully hid one chess piece in the fountain. He planned to go back for it later," said the policeman. "He was just going to put the other one in, when Mr. Grubbs walked up. So Cal only had time to get rid of one. He got on his bike and left. By then he could see no one was being searched and he thought he was home free with one of the pieces, anyway."

"But how did that chess piece get into the Birdman's bread bag?" Cindy asked.

"I bet I know," said Jay. "When Cal saw the police car stop, he thought someone had seen him take the chessmen, so he slipped the piece in the Birdman's cart, in the bag of bread."

"Right you are," said Officer Brady.

"What about Mr. Grubbs?" asked Cindy.

"I think I know now why Mr. Grubbs was mad

at us that morning," Dexter said. "It was because of the cement. That's how Mr. Grubbs knew we'd been in the park the night before. He had to patch up those footprints. He thought we must have climbed the fence because he didn't know anyone had opened the gate."

"Right again," said Hap Brady.

"But why did Mr. Grubbs lie about the museum director?" asked Cindy. "He said the director was there. But the director was really out of town."

"Because he knew the job was going to take a long time, and the director had left town without giving instructions for closing early," explained the policeman. "So Mr. Grubbs just took the responsibility of closing early to have time for the job."

"And what about Agnes Lampkins?" asked Jay.

"She's cranky, all right, and she hates kids. But she didn't really do a thing," said Hap Brady.

"But why didn't she report the theft?" asked Mr. Tate.

"Because she knew Mr. Thorndyke would be

angry about the theft but wouldn't contact the police. She didn't want to be the one to report it and maybe get in trouble with him. And she didn't want the kids to report the theft because it was her duty to do it. And she didn't want to get in trouble with the museum," said Hap Brady.

"Everything fits," said Cindy, sighing happily. "No missing pieces."

"A few missing pieces, still," said Dexter. "How did Cal Crump open the gate to the museum park, for instance?"

"Cal picked the lock," said Hap Brady. "He always does that. He can get into any place he wants."

"He can get into any place?" asked Mrs. Tate.

"Well, he *could*," said Hap Brady. "Not any longer!"

After Hap Brady left, the Tates and Temples sat around the table talking.

"I'll never make fun of your playing detectives again," said Anne.

"Until the next time," laughed Dexter.

So much had happened in one day that it was

hard for Jay and Cindy and Dexter to get to sleep that night.

The next afternoon they found the Birdman in the museum park. They could hardly wait to talk to him about the mystery.

"How did you know all along I was innocent?" the Birdman asked.

Cindy looked guiltily at the two boys. They looked back at her even more guiltily.

Jay spoke up, "We did think you were the thief, as a matter of fact," he said. "You can thank Cindy."

"Yes, she was always coming to your rescue," said Dexter.

"By the way," said Dexter. "I saw *you* put something in the fountain right after we discovered the chess pieces were missing. That's when I really started suspecting you. What was it?"

The Birdman scratched his head. "Oh, that must have been that quarter I put in. See, everyone throws pennies in for good luck. No one would bother taking a penny, right? Well, once a year the museum takes all the coins and gives them to the children's hospital. So once in a while I put in a dime or a quarter. But I like to hide them under the pennies so no one will take them. They're for the children at that hospital, see?"

"I see," said Cindy.

They all sat and tried to figure out some of the other missing pieces of the puzzle. "What about the magazine cover?" asked Dexter. "The one that was cut up for the ransom note. It had your name on it. Cal threw it on the Temples' front porch. He wanted us to find it."

"Mr. Crump saw the magazine in my cart," said the Birdman. "He seemed interested so I gave it to him. I thought he'd become a bird lover that way."

Jay said, "So everything fits. Even the dog that growled at Cal Crump. Remember Randy? The reason he growled was because Cal kicked him when he stole the ashtrays from the Peabody porch. Cal figured Randy knew him and wouldn't bark. But Randy did bark. So Cal kicked him to keep him quiet. That's why Randy growled at him the next day."

"Kicking Randy. How mean!" said Cindy.

"Yes, he was mean," said Jay. "Trying to put the blame on the Birdman. And trying to get Mr. Thorndyke to pay a ransom." He shook his head. "He told everything down at the police station. He's just been going around from one town to another, doing stuff to get extra money. He's almost always got by."

"But not this time," said Cindy, smiling. "Oh," she said to the Birdman, remembering something.

"What about those boots you threw away?"

"Oh, I was going to wash them, use them again, but then I decided they weren't worth saving. I saw you looking at my new black shoes and probably thinking my old boots were pretty worn out. So I threw out the old boots and got new ones—see?" He pointed to his new boots.

Cindy looked at the Birdman and smiled. "I just knew you couldn't have done any of those things, somehow. But so many things looked bad. What about telling us you'd never even seen a chess set?"

"I haven't," said the Birdman. "I wouldn't know one if I saw one, except that one piece that was in with the bread."

"But we saw one—a hidden box—in your storage locker. On a shelf," said Cindy.

He shook his head. "I've never seen one," he repeated.

"In a little box, a little brown box," insisted Cindy.

"Oh," said the Birdman, his eyes twinkling. "A carved box, yes. Someone gave that to me many years ago. I thought it was just some odds and ends. It looked like little dolls or something. I really never looked at them. So that's a chess set. Well, well."

Suddenly they were all startled by the sounds of loud voices in the park. Agnes Lampkins and Mr. Grubbs were standing at the fountain arguing. Her voice was shrill, and his was deep and loud. Both of them sounded very disagreeable.

Jay and Cindy and Dexter started to laugh, and the Birdman joined in. "It's so hard for some people to relax," said the Birdman finally.

Jay jumped up. "Hey, I'll be late for my paper route!" he said. "Want to come with me, Dex?"

"Oh, sure," said Dexter.

They ran off. Cindy sat with the Birdman and looked at the swans. "Isn't it funny about people?" she said. "Mr. Grubbs and Agnes Lampkins are sort of like Rose and Thorn—ornery." She sighed. "I like people like you. And swans like Albert and Einstein," she said, tossing some crusts of bread to the waiting swans.